Dickens' novels, like those of his contemporaries, are more explicitly indebted to the theatre than scholars have supposed: his stories and characters were often already public property by the time they were published, circulating as part of a current theatrical repertoire well known to many Victorian readers. In this book, Deborah Vlock argues that novels – and novel readers – were in effect created by the popular theatre in the nineteenth century, and that the possibility of reading and writing narrative was conditioned by the culture of the stage. Vlock resuscitates the long-dead voices of Dickens' theatrical sources, which now only tentatively inhabit reviews, scripts, fiction, and nonfiction narratives, but which were everywhere in Dickens' time: voices of noted actors and actresses and of popular theatrical characters. She uncovers unexpected precursors for some popular Dickensian characters, and reconstructs the conditions in which Dickens' novels were initially received.

Deborah Vlock has taught Victorian literature and culture at Brandeis University and Boston College. She is author of several articles on Victorian literature and culture, and a contributor to the *New Dictionary of National Biography*.

CAMBRIDGE STUDIES IN NINETEENTH-CENTURY
LITERATURE AND CULTURE 19

# DICKENS, NOVEL READING, AND THE VICTORIAN POPULAR THEATRE

# CAMBRIDGE STUDIES IN NINETEENTH-CENTURY LITERATURE AND CULTURE

General editors
Gillian Beer, *University of Cambridge*

Editorial board
Isobel Armstrong, *Birkbeck College, London*
Terry Eagleton, *University of Oxford*
Leonore Davidoff, *University of Essex*
Catherine Gallagher, *University of California, Berkeley*
D. A. Miller, *Columbia University*
J. Hillis Miller, *University of California, Irvine*
Mary Poovey, *New York University*
Elaine Showalter, *Princeton University*

Nineteenth-century British literature and culture have been rich fields for interdisciplinary studies. Since the turn of the twentieth century, scholars and critics have tracked the intersections and tensions between Victorian literature and the visual arts, politics, social organization, economic life, technical innovations, scientific thought – in short, culture in its broadest sense. In recent years, theoretical challenges and historiographical shifts have unsettled the assumptions of previous scholarly syntheses and called into question the terms of older debates. Whereas the tendency in much past literary critical interpretation was to use the metaphor of culture as "background," feminist, Foucauldian, and other analyses have employed more dynamic models that raise questions of power and of circulation. Such developments have reanimated the field.

This series aims to accommodate and promote the most interesting work being undertaken on the frontiers of the field of nineteenth-century literary studies: work which intersects fruitfully with other fields of study such as history, or literary theory, or the history of science. Comparative as well as interdisciplinary approaches are welcomed.

A complete list of titles published will be found at the end of the book.

# DICKENS, NOVEL READING, AND THE VICTORIAN POPULAR THEATRE

DEBORAH VLOCK

CAMBRIDGE
UNIVERSITY PRESS

PUBLISHED BY THE PRESS SYNDICATE OF THE UNIVERSITY OF CAMBRIDGE
The Pitt Building, Trumpington Street, Cambridge CB2 1RP, United Kingdom

CAMBRIDGE UNIVERSITY PRESS
The Edinburgh Building, Cambridge, CB2 2RU, United Kingdom   http://www.cup.cam.ac.uk
40 West 20th Street, New York, NY 10011–4211, USA   http://www.cup.org
10 Stamford Road, Oakleigh, Melbourne 3166, Australia

First published 1998

Printed in the United Kingdom at the University Press, Cambridge

Typeset in Baskerville 11.5/12 pt [VN]

*A catalogue record for this book is available from the British Library*

*Library of Congress cataloging-in-publication data*

Vlock, Deborah.
Dickens, novel reading, and the Victorian popular theatre/
Deborah Vlock
p.   cm.   (Cambridge Studies in Nineteenth-century Literature and Culture: 19)
Includes bibliographical references.
ISBN 0 521 64084 9
1. Dickens, Charles, 1812–1870 – Knowledge – Performing Arts.
2. Dickens, Charles, 1812–1870 – Appreciation – Great Britain.
3. Fiction – Appreciation – Great Britain – History – nineteenth century.
4. Authors and readers – Great Britain – History – nineteenth century.
5. Books and reading – Great Britain – History – nineteenth century.
6. Popular culture – Great Britain – History – nineteenth century.
7. Theatre – Great Britain – History – nineteenth century.
8. Performing Arts in literature.   I. Title.   II. Series.
PR4592.P45V58   1998   823'.8–dc21
98–21087   CIP

ISBN 0 521 64084 9 hardback

# Contents

# Illustrations

# *Acknowledgments*

This book could not have been written and revised without grants from the Society for Theatre Research, whose generous assistance enabled me to undertake research in London; the Northeast Modern Language Association; and the Louis, Frances, and Jeffrey Sachar Fund. A scholarship from a Center for Theatre Education and Research allowed me a necessary summer's study in London and Stratford. I am grateful to all four donors. Eugene Goodheart and Paul Morrison, two fine critics, dispensed advice and encouragement, without which I would too often have been lost in a maze of my own making. Raphael Seligmann and Anke Finger read drafts of chapters and made me laugh during this occasionally dispiriting undertaking. And Homer Swander, with typical generosity and enthusiasm, fostered my work in countless large and small ways; my debt to him is great, and duly noted.

Several theatre professionals donated some of their time and wisdom to this project, and I should like to thank them here. Patrick Stewart, whose *A Christmas Carol* taught me a great deal about reading and playing Dickens, shared with me what he does and how he does it; Stephen Rashbrook gave me an hour's conversation in the Duke's Head pub about the Royal Shakespeare Company's *Nicholas Nickleby*, in which he took part; John Culme shared his experience as a collector of Victorian theatre materials; and Tony Church discussed acting and literature with equal acumen and enthusiasm.

Josie Dixon and Linda Bree of Cambridge University Press walked me through a complicated process with great kindness and competence – I wish every writer such excellent editors. The staffs at the Harvard Theatre Collection and the British Library Department of Manuscripts made maneuvering through the maze of materials therein quite a bit less daunting; I thank them collectively for their patient help.

Finally, thanks to my loving family, now only three: Ruth, Richard, and Robert. Andrea always believed this book would be published but did not live to see it. My own Annika, her namesake, will perhaps read it someday instead. To Jörg Drewitz, who has shared with me some of life's sharpest pains and sweetest pleasures, I can only repeat what Mozart's Sesto confides more mellifluously to his love: *il mio destin tu sei, tutto farò per te.*

The first chapter of this book appeared previously, in a shorter version, as "Dickens, Theater, and the Making of a Victorian Reading Public," in *Studies in the Novel*, 29, 2, 1997: pp. 164–190.

# Introduction

This book comes into the world at a time when Victorian studies are dominated by the spirit of Michel Foucault, whose construction of modern European social history, with its evolution from the spectacular, public discourse of the Enlightenment to the privatized, domesticated culture of the industrial revolution, has informed a large body of exciting scholarship. This study, certainly, is indebted to *Discipline and Punish* and *Madness and Civilization*, which have enabled me to imagine and describe the structures of social differentiation and containment which operate in Victorian novels and popular entertainments.[1] But if Foucault's voice is generally present here, it is here, much of the time, to be challenged, as a voice potentially as totalizing and controlling as the cultural forces it describes. If we accept as accurate the discursive shift he defines as a more or less material cultural change occurring around the end of the eighteenth century, a shift from the spectacular to the speculative, from the corporal to the carceral, then we are led to accept as well a vision of novel reading and writing in Victorian England which emphasizes isolation, privacy, the contemplative reading subject – a reductive and romanticized view of a complex subject. Acts of novel reading and writing took place in "public spaces" – that is, in the terms of a popular agreement, a framework of consensual cultural ideas and the signs assumed to represent those ideas – in the nineteenth century, even when performed in isolation and silence. Novel reading literally entered the public sphere when novelists like Dickens took to the platform and performed public readings, and, less obviously, when the novels themselves borrowed heavily from the theatre, employing almost casually, and with confidence in their readers' collective understanding, some of the standard theatrical signs of the time.

This is not to say that an attention to the inward, the carceral, the embracing structures of control operating in nineteenth-century Europe is uninteresting or invalid. Indeed, this book enthusiastically examines

Victorian social controls, performing readings which might well be described as "Foucauldian" themselves. But I wish to turn the carceral cell inside out, to expose the very public nature of the Victorian hegemony. In other words, I object not to the assumption that the nineteenth century moved to bourgeois rhythms, or was buried under layers of ideology, but to an unexamined belief in the interiority of modern culture. A number of scholars have embraced that idea, and produced suggestive but perhaps short-sighted treatments of nineteenth-century novels and novel readers. D. A. Miller may be the most prominent among them, and while *The Novel and the Police* remains among the most successful books on the subject, it almost ruthlessly appropriates Victorian novels and their readers, packaging both entities in cells, if you will, of its own construction, and locking its doors against alternative treatments.

Since the novel counts among the conditions for [its] consumption the consumer's leisured withdrawal to the private, domestic sphere, then every novel-reading subject is constituted – willy-nilly, and almost before he has read a word – within the categories of the individual, the inward, the domestic. There is no doubt that the shift in the dominant literary form from the drama to the novel at the end of the seventeenth century had to do with the latter's superior efficacy in producing and providing for privatized subjects.[2]

This passage engages in a critical policing of its own: it is difficult to resist the assertion that the reading subject is constituted implicitly, even "naturally" – "willy-nilly, and almost before he has read a word" – within the categories Miller has devised for him. But if we do resist, if we entertain the possibility that the nineteenth century, despite its privileging of the inward and private, perceived itself in other ways as well – published its image, its values, its desires, in extravagantly public venues like the theatre, and depended on such publicity to promote a discourse which favored "interiority" – then it is less clear than Miller suggests that the shift in the dominant literary form, from drama to fiction, was due to the novel's greater efficacy in constituting the private subject, or indeed, that this shift occurred at all.

The primary assumption behind this study is that Foucault's historical model performs the same discursive function it describes, totalizing and containing nineteenth-century culture in a way that renders it *readable* to the twentieth century, but which erases its very strong spectacular, externalizing impulses. This paradigm does not adequately express the differences between early modern and modern cultures; it polarizes them without considering certain inevitable complications in the constructed binarism, the moments, for example, when nineteenth-century Europe recognizes itself through publicly displayed bodies, or the prototypical carceral imaginations of certain early European writers, like Tommaso Campanella (*La Città del Sole*, 1623). One way to think of the present study's theoretical position is to imagine it conversing with Foucault, but also with Bakhtin, whose "dialogic" novel reverberates with theatrical voices, a more public entity than the one permitted by Foucault's vision, but subject to the same hegemonizing desires described in *Discipline and Punish*. Foucault has taught us how to recognize the structures of social control – this book, certainly, has benefitted from the lesson – but Bakhtin had already, preemptively, as it works out, demonstrated how such controls are constantly subverted by the nineteenth century's irrepressible heteroglossia. I wish my argument to encompass both possibilities, the Bakhtinian (discursive regulation which generally fails) and the Foucauldian (discursive regulation which generally succeeds), privileging neither one but finding each useful at one time or another. In every instance, however, I shall insist upon the primacy of public display, a phenomenon which Foucault has associated with pre-industrial Europe but which continued to be a powerful organizing and controlling force through the nineteenth century, and indeed, continues to do its work in our century as well.

Some of the strongest evidence for this continuity lies in the popular entertainments of nineteenth-century England. As this book hopes to demonstrate, the tropes of the theatre gave voice to other forms of artistic and popular expression; people read novels, newspapers, social criticism – indeed, just about everything worth reading – through the lens of popular performance. In other words, the "drama" was not supplanted by the novel in the nineteenth century but merged with it, enabling the novel to exist. Dickens, who figures at the center of this study, regularly borrowed characters, dramatic idioms, even stories from the melodrama, and the popular theatre borrowed equally from him; the same may be said for many of his contemporaries.[3] What this means is that the Victorian novel did not really resemble the discrete textual unit we receive it as today, the self-contained package Miller imagines as privately and personally consumed, but was loose and fluid – particularly when published serially, as so many novels, including Dickens', were – and attentive to the theatrical developments which were at once its source and its competition. That Dickens' novels were so often adapted and produced before he had finished writing them raises some interesting and exciting questions about the role of theatre and performance in their composition. For example, when adapters like Edward Stirling or W. T. Moncrieff devised what seemed a probable ending to one of the novels, so that it could be quickly produced, what effect did that have on the ending Dickens ultimately wrote? He hated most of the adaptations of his novels, but he appears to have followed them carefully. The probability that novelists, like Dickens, whose serial fiction was regularly plagiarized, were forced to dance with hack play-wrights as they wrote, requires us to rethink our relationship to these texts.

If we imagine the novel and the drama as intimately conversant with each other, rather than in binary relation or in chronological sequence with drama the genre of early modern culture, and the novel, which supersedes it, the product of full-blooded modernity, we must likewise imagine a reading subject constituted otherwise than in the interior spaces of home and privatized imagination. This is what I have under-taken in this book: a repositioning of the Victorian bourgeois reading subject, a re-visioning of the Victorian novel, and a recovery of the conditions in which both novels and novel readers were made.

At the center of this study lies the theatre, lively, healthy, magnificently vocal – not a thing of the past but an integral part of the Victorian present. One should perhaps avoid the use of the word *drama* in describing the genre of writing produced for the stage, because it implies a literariness which popular Victorian plays emphatically lacked. These were often colorful, inelegant vocal-spectacular displays, written in and for a virtual moment, and significant now primarily for their significance then. That significance was substantial: the popular theatre mediated acts of novel reading and writing, structured class and gender relationships, informed political discourse, and entered the fields of journalism and social science, providing small- and large-scale models of relationship.

Several recent works on nineteenth-century fiction and theatre pro-ved to be indispensable to this project. D. A. Miller's *The Novel and the Police* and *Narrative and its Discontents* articulated some of the novel's important regulating functions, like its self-policing and its understand-ing of generic and discursive imperatives, and despite my arguments with Miller's construction of the Victorian novel and reader as ultimate-ly privatized entities, I could not have formulated my own position without his, against which this study differentiates itself.[4] Martin Meisel's *Realizations*,[5] far grander than this book aspires to be, articulates the intersections among the arts that I have presumed here. Joseph Litvak's *Caught in the Act: Theatricality in the Nineteenth-Century English Novel* says a great deal about Victorian attitudes towards the theatre, and about the positioning of otherness – particularly homosexuality and femaleness – within performative or theatrical and narrative apparati.[6] Litvak's study "repeatedly emphasizes the *normalization* of theatricality, its subtle diffusion throughout the culture that would appear to have repudiated it . . . [and shows] how, if theatrical structures and techniques underlie or enable various coercive cultural mechanisms, the same structures and techniques can threaten those mechanisms' smooth functioning" (pp. x–xi). These are ideas underlying this work as well, which implies many of the conclusions of Litvak's study even when it, perhaps ungratefully, challenges or rejects some of his premises – especially those Foucauldian-inspired assumptions which I find so insufficiently circumspect, or permissive, to accommodate all of the facets of Victorian experience.

Much has been written over the past twenty years or so on the Victorian theatre, and while almost all of it is valuable in one way or another, this body of criticism tends to be motivated by narrative concerns, reading theatre and theatricality narrativistically, and linking the novel and other popular forms to the theatre biographically or anecdotally. (Two notable exceptions are George Taylor's *Players and Performances in the Victorian Theatre*, and Joseph Roach's *The Player's Passion*.[7]) In other words, literary scholarship has typically imagined "theatre" – a phenomenon, in the nineteenth century, only nominally literary but overwhelmingly vocal, gestural, spectacular – to be synonymous with "drama," and has sought in it the narrative structures which underlie realist fiction, reading its relationships to the social and literary worlds as one reads novels, chronologically, sequentially; relying on literary interpretive strategies, on the existence of the signifying properties typically found in written text. This suggests, more than anything, that we, as readers and writers, are constituted narratively rather than theatrically; that our organizing apparatus "naturally" constructs our experience in linear, chronological sequence, presuming logical, "storied" relationships. In this we differ from the Victorians, who understood their theatre, their literature, even their social world, in terms of very explicit non-narrative signs (voices, postures) as well as the stories which tied those signs into narrative units. Still, the work of scholars like Nina Auerbach, Philip Collins, Michael Booth, George Rowell, Edwin Eigner, Robert Garis, and others has shown that the nineteenth-century English theatre is a legitimate and exciting topic of discussion, and the present study has profited from them.[8]

In order to evoke acts of Victorian novel-reading and writing – and to some extent, the everyday performances of Victorian life – I have had to imagine a world in which reading took place under different circumstances than it does today; a world laced with glittery threads of theatricality, in which voices and physical gestures crowded the imagination, haunting the reading and writing subject. (Although this study primarily examines the influence of the theatre on novel writing and reading, it often draws on the other art forms – music, painting, and illustration, for example – which exerted a similar influence, as Meisel's expansive *Realizations* has shown us.) The fact of these "hauntings" is suggested in the novels and theatrical entertainments themselves; I had merely to learn how to experience them, to hear the theatrical voices and rhythms blended into fictional narratives. This was less difficult than one might imagine. Reading aloud had always been a part of my literary experience; my father read to me all of Dickens' novels, some more than once, from my early years in primary school through college, and I continue to explore spoken text as a regular part of literary interpretation. In reading Dickens aloud, one finds certain rhythmic and inflective patterns and quite "naturally" finds a series of dramatic voices at one's disposal. His texts require this, and somehow make it happen. I suggest that we read Victorian novels aloud as a matter of course – the Victorians did – if we wish to recover them in their authentic forms.

But imagining how Victorian novels sounded, felt, and tasted to the nineteenth century requires more than acts of oral reading. It requires acts of exploration, imagination, and reconstruction. In order to describe successfully the atmosphere in which English novels were produced and consumed I have had to coin a phrase: *imaginary text*. I wish "imaginary text" to resonate with similar constructions by other cultural theorists – Paul Davis' "culture text" is one of the first to come to mind[9] – but to emphasize, with its insistence on imagination, the tenuous distinction between "reality" and theatre or fiction which distinguishes, as I shall argue, the nineteenth century. "Imaginary text" should suggest a "reading space" located outside of the actual narrative embodiments of Victorian novels, and inside the field of sociodramatic possibilities – of idioms and gestures and a whole range of signifiers – established by popular entertainments. Victorian novel readers read in this space; both they and their novels were born into an agreement – written, as it were, in the language of theatricality – about certain types of character and story. Restoring some of these agreements or imaginary texts has enabled me to approximate, in my own readings, the very aural and spectacular act of Victorian reading, and it has tuned my ears to the voices, conventional but deeply powerful, which sang in printed narrative text – particularly Dickens' text.

The following chapters attempt to share that recovery, to demonstrate how the nineteenth-century novel fitted into its own historical moment, and how the recently popular interpretive paradigms fail to adequately express the nature of that moment. There have been certain difficulties inherent in this project, because our historical moment has integrated the structures of narrative so deeply into its framework that the critical language available to describe Victorian theatricality always seems to imply narrativistic or novelistic relationships. Still, it is possible to peer through the inevitable cracks in the foundation, at a world perhaps more foreign than we have liked to think, and to watch it go about its business of knowing itself and knowing others.

# CHAPTER 2

# Dickens and the "imaginary text"

Nineteenth-century English fiction has undergone a certain transformation at the hands of twentieth-century critics, who have read Victorian
novels in discrete critical editions and assumed them to be privatized
narrative expressions of modern bourgeois subjectivity.[1] While it is true
that something which might be called a "bourgeois subjectivity" evolved in the nineteenth century, it is less than certain that the privatized
subjectivity which has been so frequently invoked by cultural theorists
sufficiently describes the nineteenth-century imagination. Nor does D.
A. Miller's totalizing claim that "the novel counts among the conditions
for [its] consumption the consumer's leisured withdrawal to the private,
domestic sphere, [and hence] every novel-reading subject is constituted
– willy-nilly, and almost before he has read a word – within the
categories of the individual, the inward, the domestic"[2] adequately
describe either the nineteenth-century novel or its readers, both of
which took their form, as it were, in a culture characterized equally by
theatrical and public, as well as domestic and private, impulses.

If we entertain the possibility that the nineteenth century, despite its
significantly circumscribed or internalized institutions, understood itself
in other ways – aural and spectacular ways, for example; as a theatre of
voices and figures – then we are forced to question some of the assumptions currently circulating about nineteenth-century literature and culture: for example, that the novel replaced the drama as dominant
literary form, and that the ascendency of the private subject prompted
this change. This study disputes those assumptions and the Foucauldian
paradigm supporting them: that is, the presumption of a historical
evolution from the spectacularity of early modern Europe to the intro-
spectiveness of fully fledged modernity. This shift, if we accept it uncon-
ditionally, imposes upon the nineteenth-century novel the burden of an
intense privacy, an internally driven economy, and a consumption by
individuals in the domestic enclosures which constitute their homes. I

would describe this construction of the Victorian novel and novel reader as burdensome because it relentlessly denies the possibility of other kinds of reading and writing, including that which I maintain was peculiarly Victorian: a reading and writing mediated by the popular theatre.[3]

The Victorian reading subject did not resemble the solitary, withdrawn figure Miller has imagined for us,[4] but performed his or her reading in a highly public "space," drawing upon a set of consensual popular assumptions, cultural stereotypes regularly published on the stage and generally accepted as representative of Victorian social reality. In other words, Victorian readings were mediated by the culture of theatre – not merely because reading so often took the form of public declamation in the nineteenth century, although activities of this sort have been well documented,[5] but because novelists like Dickens drew quite freely from the body of sociodramatic possibilities established by the theatre, using theatrical tropes with an evident confidence in their familiarity to readers.

The end to which my disassembling of certain privileged critical structures aspires is a recovery of Victorian novels, particularly the novels of Dickens; a situation of these novels in their original contexts, and a reconstruction of the conditions in which they were initially received. Such recovery is, however, fraught with a certain danger – the danger of seeking the nineteenth century and finding only our highly self-conscious selves. Herbert Blau has shown how the recovery of the past, say in period dramas, is always about ourselves, a "reconstitut[ion] of ourselves, for instance, as the audience of Greek tragedy,"[6] or more appropriately, here, the audience of nineteenth-century melodrama. If looking for the past inevitably means turning up the disappointment, merely, of a hyper-aware present, ourselves in stays and stocks and morning coats – and that is possibly the best we can hope for – then recovering the Victorian novel requires most of all a readerly shift: we must transform ourselves into "Victorian" readers, and if we are lucky, the novels will follow. This will require that we change our relationship to these texts, that we entertain the possibility that a Dickens novel is not exclusively (and privately) literary, but expresses itself in three dimensions, so to speak; visually and vocally as well as narratively. We may perhaps achieve this "new" relationship by reading aloud, or at least with an attention to strains of voice, in order to hear the rhythms, inflections, accents, and vocal cadences which resonate through the novels. However we do it, it will require a substantial amount of imagination: we can only reinstate the conditions under which Dickens' novels lived, and resuscitate the long-dead voices of his theatrical sources, by learning to experience them, somehow, in our own heads. These voices, which now only tentatively inhabit Victorian reviews, scripts, fiction, and nonfiction narratives, were everywhere in Dickens' time, the voices of particular actors and actresses, popular characters, even the novelist himself. When Dickens' characters spoke, they sounded familiar – they had already been circulating as part of the standard theatrical repertoire by the time he wrote his novels. In this respect he is less original than we might like to think.

Theatrical borrowing, on Dickens' part at least, has been discussed fairly extensively, but little or no attention has been paid to the role that theatre played in the formation of a reading public in nineteenth-century England, and no significant piece of scholarship has adequately explored the generic questions raised by this commerce between novel and stage. Some critics, like Paul Schlicke,[7] locate Dickens' novels in their theatrical contexts but never question the authority of genre, ultimately privileging the novels' life outside of the theatrical, their literary autonomy, if you will, and merely noting their structural and thematic similarities to the popular entertainments which influenced them. This is a fairly typical take on Dickens' fiction, but it presumes disciplinary or generic divisions which, although in theory quintessentially Victorian, did not in fact exist with much integrity in the nineteenth century. Novels and theatrical entertainments, novels and journalistic prose, novels and poetry constantly slipped in and out of mutual embrace. Henry Mayhew's *London Labour and the London Poor* influenced scores of novels and plays, no less than other novels and plays had shaped Mayhew's imagination. Poems like Robert Browning's *The Ring and the Book* and Elizabeth Barrett Browning's *Aurora Leigh* adopted novelistic gestures. And the contemporary stage provided material for novels, which themselves generously reciprocated, so that the lines between theatre and prose fiction were fluid, and novel reading was performed in the rich and ambiguous area in between.

Hence, while Dickens borrowed from the theatre, he also contributed to it: virtually all his novels were adapted for the stage as quickly as he turned them out – often, indeed, before the last installments were published. In this way many of his readers received multiple versions simultaneously: the novel itself as it came out in monthly numbers, and the staged adaptations which reduced characters and plots to conventional types, but lent specific sounds and shapes to Dickens' written text.[8] This affected the way that Victorians read not only Dickens, but generally speaking the fiction of their era, most of which drew in some way or other from the theatre, and much of which found its way on to the stage during its period of active circulation.[9] If this study focuses primarily on Dickens and neglects some of the other Victorian novelists who trafficked in the theatre, it is partly because his connection to the theatre is more explicit than theirs, his sources more directly available, and partly because, in this universe of quasi-successful treatments of theatricality in the works of this most theatrical of novelists, another attempt is warranted.

The relationship between novel and theatre was a fairly complex symbiosis, complicated particularly by an obscurance of origin, an absence of fixedness in either of the genres which would allow us to cite, with absolute confidence, one of them as the primary genre. But I do, in spite of this originary ambiguity, presume a basic source for novels in the English theatre which is not always or necessarily reciprocal, a position which may be justified by the fact that novelists like Dickens supplied the *contemporary* theatre with specific material, but theatrical influence on English culture and narrative was already of long duration by the nineteenth century, and the theatre's contributions to narrative were as often semiotic and structural as they were plot-related or ideological. Wherever one locates the original – and I will sometimes suggest theatre as a novel source, sometimes as one of several complementary elements of the cultural script which enabled Victorian reading – the more or less explicit theatrical influence on the novel suggests that Victorian readers, at least those who also went to the theatre, or were versed in the current theatrical culture, experienced Dickens differently than how we do today; their reading was complicated by theatrical renditions which contracted and corrupted plots, and reduced characters to basic dramatic types. Out of the concords and discords of these competing texts evolved what I would call an "imaginary text" – the actual Dickens experience, overdetermined, centered not so much in any one narrative or genre but in the theatre of assumptions circulating among the London public.

Dickens, perhaps more than any of his contemporaries, was a collective idea – public property in the most absolute sense. His characters and plots filled Victorian imaginations. People read him with a strong faith in his truth and originality, and a simultaneous conviction that they personally knew his characters. Obviously we cannot, receiving Dickens as essentially literary, reproduce this Victorian reading experience in an authentic way; this unfortunate problem has troubled me many times in the course of writing this book, which takes as its subject so much Victorian ephemera, the long-dead popular entertainments which were, in their time, such a powerful cultural force. But we can examine for ourselves the multiple "Dickens texts" – novels, plays, actors, reviews – that resounded in the Victorian reader's head, and imagine what sort of larger collective text they made together.

This study will eventually turn to comic, specifically pattered, voices in Dickens, and has located, in several instances, verbal and character-ological prototypes for some of his most famous comic characters, theatrical figures which the novelist picked up, consciously or not, from the stage, and which I have striven to see and "hear" as Victorian readers did. My conviction that many of Dickens' characters came to him from the theatre[10] has encouraged me to listen for dramatic voices in his fiction, the same voices which were, in fact, current on the stage and resonant in the Victorian imagination, circulating as conventional verbal stereotypes among the London public.[11] This listening is aided by my own literary history. I was fortunate enough to have a parent who read to me, from a very early age, most of Dickens, and I still hear – perhaps faintly now, but truly – strains of real voices in his novels, the characters as my father spoke them. One cannot emphasize enough the importance of reading these texts aloud, to establish the vocal rhythms and cadences that Dickens placed in them. When we do this, they take on life, they become organic, spontaneously generating dramas, and we become active participants in a peculiar kind of creative process – a making of theatre. Contemporary readers of Dickens recognized this. One Victorian critic described this agency of the reading subject in painterly terms, the student's or draftsman's coloring-in:

Mr. Dickens' characters are sketched with a spirit and distinctness which rarely fail to convey immediately a clear impression of the person intended. They are, however, not complete and finished delineations, but rather outlines, very clearly and sharply traced, which the reader may fill up for himself.[12]

The fact that the reader may fill up the outlines for himself in a way that enhances or finishes the author's "impression" suggests that the reading public shared a set of ideas about character, ideas which enabled them to complete the picture. This implication of the reading subject in performance is crucial to recovering the Victorian Dickens; so too is a willingness to broaden the very concept of performance to include that which happens in social interaction, to look outside of the act of reading and into the larger and looser act of living for traces of the performative. As Paul Campbell has written,

far from limiting dramatic discourse to literature, [one should] consider it as the dimension of language in which we create and recreate ourselves in relation to the "real" world around us and in which we use those imaginative or artistic events . . . to become new beings or personae.[13]

Dickens constantly "created and recreated" himself in relation to the outside world, experimenting with voices and personae in life as he did in narrative. He also, of course, read from his works in public, using them as vehicles for his own dramatic voice. He saw his novels as strains of dialogue, and of dialogic descriptive prose, to be spoken and heard, to be invented and reinvented at each reading.

It is no coincidence that one of the most successful Dickens adaptations of this century, the Royal Shakespeare Company's *Nicholas Nickleby* (1980), was conceived, written, and produced as the result of a series of workshops in which the company, directors, and writer took turns reciting, analyzing, and performing chapters from the novel.[14] Out of this polylogue evolved a concept for turning Dickens into theatre. Speech, in *Nickleby,* is a social and dramatic agent, a force that creates people and stories, polyvalent, interactive, constantly forming and re-forming the novel's socio-aesthetic reality; the RSC's production recognizes that, and it begins with a collection of dialogic speeches, setting the stage for a play that is about, at least as much as anything else, the resonance and relationships in human voices.

*As the audience come in, the Company mingles with them, welcoming them to the show. Eventually, the whole company assembles on stage. Each member of the company takes at least one of the lines of the opening narration.*
NARRATION. There once lived in a sequestered part of the county of Devonshire, one Mr. Godfrey Nickleby, who, rather late in life, took it into his head to get married.

And in due course, when Mrs. Nickleby had presented her husband with two sons, he found himself in a situation of distinctly shortened means,

Which were only relieved when, one fine morning, there arrived a black-bordered letter, informing him that his uncle was dead and left him the bulk of his property, amounting in all to five thousand pounds.

And with a portion of this property, Mr. Godfrey Nickleby purchased a small farm near Dawlish,

And on his death . . . he was able to leave to his eldest son three thousand pounds in cash, and to his youngest, three thousand and the farm.

The younger boy was of a timid and retiring disposition . . .

The elder son, however, resolved to make much use of his father's inheritance.

. . .

And while Ralph prospered in the mercantile way in London, the younger brother lived still on the farm,

And took himself a wife,

Who gave birth to a boy and a girl,

And by the time they were both nearing the age of twenty, he found his expenses much increased and his capital still more depleted.

Speculate. His wife advised him.

Think of your brother, Mr. Nickleby, and speculate.

And Mr. Nickleby did speculate,

But a mania prevailed,

A bubble burst,

. . .

Four hundred nobodies were ruined,

And one of them was

Mr. Nickleby.[15]

As lines were distributed among the actors, the group seems to have made an interesting discovery: if they gave those lines referring to certain characters to the characters themselves, they could reproduce on the stage a gesture peculiar to fictional narrative – the endowment of third-person narrative with specific character consciousness, so that the objective voice temporarily takes on subjective dimensions. In other words, the actress playing Mrs. Nickleby, the actor playing her brother-in-law Ralph, become narrator for a moment, uttering those lines attributed to them by the narrative as well as those referring to them. Throughout the play, each voice (the novel is full of them) is rung in this way against the others, the authoritative, ironic, comic, sentimental, in contrapuntal dialogue, and thus the dramatic text draws its audience into its rhythms and cadences in much the same way as the novel, exquisitely timed and choreographed, does its readers. This is partly because David Edgar's script is so beautifully tuned to Dickens' music, and partly because the Royal Shakespeare Company found "a way of collective storytelling that did not intrude on the internal movement of the plot, characters and incident . . . [and created] a fully rhythmic script, almost like a musical score, to facilitate an improved reading of key words and phrases."[16] They also found a way – to the extent that this is possible for a late twentieth-century acting troupe performing a contemporary script – to tap into the extratextual, the "imaginary" Dickens, the layers of voice and texture and visual image which constitute this more authentic Dickensian text. They achieved this by using mime, for example, to recover, in a form palatable to twentieth-century audiences, the physical posturing which was an integral part of Victorian theatre,[17] as well as by reproducing to the best of their abilities the standard voices of the nineteenth-century stage.

Of course, Victorian adaptations of the novel do not in any textual or conceptual way resemble David Edgar's, but my contention that the Royal Shakespeare Company took his script and turned it into a "Victorian" theatrical event is supported both by Edgar's text and their performance of that text. Given that expectations brought by late twentieth-century audiences to the theatre differ from those of their Victorian predecessors, and that late twentieth-century plays take accordingly different forms, this *Nickleby* adaptation has managed to identify and exploit some of the theatrical elements that were basic to the Victorian theatre. In spite of its patently non-Victorian structure and assumptions (Edgar's adaptation does not, for example, modify Dickens' dialogue to conform with accepted melodramatic speech acts, nor does it underscore the triumph of good over evil as starkly as the Victorian adaptations do), this dramatization of the novel explores the resonance of physical and vocal gestures, using tableaux to emphasize themes or relationships; using words and voices as explicit signifiers of social and moral position.

For example, the speech patterns of Edgar's marginalized characters announce, unambiguously, the social status of their speakers in a manner that seems "genuinely" Victorian. The disenfranchised, the uncultured, the morally corrupt use speech that deviates from the standard idiom of the narration and the play's middle-class protagonists. The little inmates of Dotheboys Hall, for example, almost always clip their sentences or separate their words with long, anxious pauses that dramatize their intellectual impoverishment, their social degradation, their physical deprivation. As if they had never received all the parts of English speech – their package was missing half its verbs, predicates, conjunctions – they utter little semantic parcels, untied, half empty, as disempowered in what they say as in how they live. At their daily roll call they create themselves in the act of self-nomination: "Twelfth. Roberts. Ten. There's something wrong – my brain" (Edgar, "Life and Adventures," p. 358). Numbers, names, deviancies – these children speak a language meaningful only in the context of Dotheboys Hall, specific to their social, economic, and physical placement in the Victorian universe.

In this sense, the play achieves its goal of resurrecting certain elements of Victorian life and theatre experience. The semiotic codes of the nineteenth-century theatre referenced real life, as we shall see, and the verbal gesturing which was one of those codes was deeply significant to the reading and theatregoing public. The urban working class, single middle-class women, gamblers, and bourgeois men, to name a few, were imagined to speak languages "naturally" appropriate to their social conditions. In *Nickleby*, Dickens himself inscribes the boys' marginality in their voices – or rather, in their lack of voice, for as a whole they exist primarily in narrative description, their silence deafening in a novel scored with hundreds of voices. But this is merely an inversion of the Victorian principle appropriated by Edgar: speak and the world knows you.

Like Dickens, Edgar invokes all of his dramatic world's social conditions in dialogue: the narrator's poetic diction (Dickens' narrative has been broken into slightly irregular blank-verse lines) suggests a high moral and aesthetic inclination; Lord Frederick Verisopht's conventional aristocratic slang, his drawling, indecisive sentences, enact his moral and physical torpor. While some of Edgar's dialogue is explicitly indebted to Dickens', much is his own invention, built partly on conventional Victorian speech patterns and partly on late twentieth-century theatrical idioms. Whatever its etiology, his characters' speech was imaginable to him, no doubt, because he knew his Victorian literature.

And knowing – that is, hearing and seeing in its various social contexts – one's Victorian literature is precisely the way to develop the most authentic relationship to it. Edgar and the RSC read Dickens aloud, to learn how to "hear" him and then "authentically" render his text. I do not mean to suggest here that a Victorian theatrical event lay waiting to erupt from Dickens' text, that Edgar had only to make minor adjustments to loose the authentic *Nickleby* play from its narrative bondage. Rather, I would argue that the play's generative process, which included reading the novel aloud, experimenting with types of performance, and watching a peculiarly vital "theatre" evolve, was a Victorian kind of process, and approximates the way that Victorian people read novels.

Dickens believed that "good" readers used the stage as their frame of reference, and that in turn, educated theatre audiences drew on their literary experiences in assessing performances. In a review of his friend William Macready in the role of Benedick, he asserts

it is not heresy to say that many people unconsciously form their opinion of such a creation as *Benedick*, not so much from the exercise of their own judgement in reading the play, as from what they have seen bodily presented to them on the stage . . . Those who consider [Macready's performance] broad, or farcical, or overstrained, cannot surely have considered all the train and course of circumstances leading up to that place. If they take them into reasonable account, and try to imagine for a moment how any master of fiction would have described *Benedick's* behaviour at that crisis – supposing it had been impossible to contemplate the appearance of a living man in the part, and therefore necessary to describe it at all – can they arrive at any other conclusion than that such ideas as are here presented by Mr. Macready would have been written down? Refer to any passage in any play of Shakespeare's, where it has been necessary to describe, as occurring beyond the scene, the behaviour of a man in a situation of ludicrous perplexity; and by that standard alone (to say nothing of any mistaken notion of natural behaviour that may have suggested itself at any time to Goldsmith, Swift, Fielding, Smollett, Sterne, Scott, or other such unenlightened journeymen) criticise, if you please, this portion of Mr. Macready's admirable performance.[18]

The most interesting effect of this defense is what might seem to late twentieth-century readers as a collapsing of the differences between "theatre" and "literature." (Victorian readers would have perceived things differently; they did not share our confidence in the separability of the two genres.) Macready's characterization is confirmed by Shakespeare's text, which is itself, by implication, elucidated by Macready's performance. His acting method, apparently contentious, may be tested against the great novels of English life and manners, with performance and novels both faithful to the model of everyday life. Novels and theatre, in other words, have equal access to the real, the genuine. Interestingly, while Dickens' intention in this review is to criticize a theatre public that has not read the original, whose only frame of reference is other performances, he himself demonstrates a reluctance to privilege the literary over the theatrical, refusing here to differentiate what is on the stage from what is in the book. For Dickens, it is not that ignorance of the literary original violates some natural generic hier-archy, but rather that an organic connection exists between the original, be it play or novel, and its theatrical manifestation. Failure to recognize that connection, not hearing the dialogue between Shakespeare's Ben-edick and Macready's Benedick, impoverishes the theatrical and/or novel-reading experience.

The theatrical mode of reading implied here is peculiarly appropriate to Dickens because he himself was committed to the exploration of human voices, to "doing 'all the voices' of his characters in his public readings" and in his personal life;[19] because he lived in a world ordered on the basis of accents and idioms; and perhaps most importantly, because his genre was so intimate with the stage. His own social prejudices, and those of his peers, were largely based on a collective agreement about verbal gesture, about how various social groups speak and what they have to say. English society is built on voices, with volumes of social history inscribed in the accents, inflections, vocabu-laries of English speech. This was certainly true in the nineteenth century, when the language was changing along with political and economic structures. These changes did not democratize speech: it mattered deeply to Dickens and his contemporaries that verbal differen-ces existed, that the Arthur Clennams of the world spoke one way, and the Jeremiah Flintwinches another. All forms of Victorian popular entertainment presumed this clear delineation of social idioms: jokes and tragedies alike were based on the voices of poverty or eccentricity striking discordant against the voices of bourgeois prosperity.

These circulating voices constituted a part of what I have called the "imaginary text."[20] Victorian novel readers read in this "imaginary" space; when they picked up any contemporary narrative they entered a sort of hybrid novelistic–theatrical genre, not plain written text but a living, theatrical dialogue between complex and stereotyped voices, between "realist" and transparently conventional stories. In other words, both they and their novels were born into an agreement about certain types of character and story, an agreement habitually dramatized – and thus in a practical sense formed – upon the English stage. Tracy Davis has noted such collective agreement in the erotic codings of the Victorian theatre, signs which enabled an audience – particularly its male members – to read the highly sexualized contexts in which actresses performed.[21] And Martin Meisel's landmark study, *Realizations*, demonstrates the phenomenon with numerous examples of the ways in which the signifiers of painting, theatre, and prose fiction cross over generic boundaries, forming a cultural text upon which popular culture consumers drew in processing their aesthetic experiences. He cites, for example, scripts which call for tableaux vivants based on popular contemporary paintings, and paintings which use the narrative tropes generally found in novels, finding some of the same stock postures and gestures in all three modes of expression: painting, fiction, and theatre. Meisel does not devote much attention to the broader sociocultural implications of such intergeneric play, which in fact offer some interesting insights into the formation of a collective Victorian social consciousness, but his work confirms that the consumers of popular culture shared a peculiar conceptual framework, a set of assumptions about human relations and behaviors which derived specifically, if not exclusively, from these three aesthetic forms. *Realizations* makes clear, in other words, that the Victorian reading/viewing subject was situated within an infinitely rich and resonant signifying universe, a subject space which one might profitably describe as "liminoid," after Victor Turner[22] – that is, a space, usually imagined as performative, as in theatrical entertainments, where creative or experimental or subversive ideas are generated. This construction appropriately posits the reader as player, since it is not merely the entertainment, as Turner would have it, but the consumer of entertainments as well who occupies that space where new ideas are activated and the prevailing discourse is either embraced or subverted.

Jürgen Habermas describes a similar "space" in early French and English bourgeois cultures, a private–public consciousness shaped by literary and artistic discourses. "In seventeenth-century France, *le public* meant the *lecteurs*, *spectateurs*, and *auditeurs* as the addressees and consumers, and the critics of art and literature."[23] This, of course, is a different public from the Victorian novel-reading and playgoing public, but Habermas discerns in it the seeds of that collective imagination which enables a diverse society to read and understand the same novels, to attend the same plays. It was the commodification of art which initially made this possible. The opening of public museums, concert halls, and theatres "institutionalized the lay judgement on art: discussion became the medium through which people appropriated art" (*Structural Transformation*, p. 40). By the nineteenth century, theatrical entertainment was itself a form of public discussion, a shared discourse, a song which everyone could hum, or could at least recognize if someone else hummed it. Early in the century Henry Siddons explained, with specific reference to "rhetorical gesture," how this integration of ideas may occur:

You tell me, that everything which is executed by *prescribed rules* will be *formal, stiff, embarrassed* and *precise*. You will please to observe how I endeavor to answer this objection. While the rule is perpetually present to the mind of the scholar, he will, perhaps, be awkward and confused in all his gestures, and the fear of making constant mistakes will render him more constrained and irresolute than if he were to give way to his habitual actions. I will grant you thus much with great willingness, but you will in return allow *me* one grand and general position, viz. that use is a second nature . . . should you state, in reply to this, that the same argument will hold good in the mere *exercise* of the profession of an actor, I answer, that though the general rule be allowed, that habit becomes a kind of nature.[24]

For the first generation of readers consuming Dickens' novels, "habit" had long since become "nature"; they already acknowledged the popular styles, characters, images – that is, the "theatre" – upon which he drew in writing as fact. When his novels appeared, the reading and theatre public automatically received them in theatrical context, as novels with one foot, so to speak, on the boards.

We can learn something about this shared context by consulting acting manuals of the period. Siddons' manual asserts that "the gestures are the exterior and visible signs of our bodies, by which the interior modifications of the soul are manifested and made known."[25] The ideas upon which Siddons draws are old – one can certainly trace them to Descartes[26] – but they prevailed upon the English stage at least through the end of the nineteenth century.[27] Today, by and large, we have lost them: Meisel points out that our own conviction that the emotions are "naturally" internal and inexpressible is a recent innovation.[28] It was certainly foreign to Dickens, who usually plants signifiers of their spiritual condition on his characters' bodies and faces, as in this description of Ralph Nickleby and his young nephew:

The face of the old man was stern, hard-featured and forbidding; that of the young one, open, handsome, and ingenuous. The old man's eye was keen with the twinklings of avarice and cunning; the young man's, bright with the light of intelligence and spirit . . . *there was an emanation from the warm young heart in his look and bearing* which kept the old man down.[29]

And Dickens is not alone among the novelists. Eliot's Felix Holt bears the "stamp of culture" on his face, while "the grandeur of his full yet firm mouth, and the calm clearness of his grey eyes," next to his rustic dress and "massive" head and neck,[30] denote a certain wholesome masculinity, identifying him for Victorian readers as the noble peasant-hero type, of which Adam Bede is another, and which turned up frequently in melodramas. Even Charlotte Brontë, whose interest in interiors, in the anguish of psychological and emotional conflict, results in novels which are less explicitly theatrical than Dickens' or even Eliot's, assumes that the very passions which consistently defy repression may be read, in novels and in life, as they are at the theatre, upon the person – physical signifiers like Bertha's bloated, purple face and St. John Rivers' "nostril, his mouth, his brow, which . . . indicated elements within either restless, or hard, or eager."[31] As Michael Booth suggests, "The expression of the face [in acting] was appropriate to the use of gesture; emotion had to be obviously visible in the countenance."[32] Externalized in this way, moral character and even details of plot could be apprehended semiotically, read on the faces or in the gestures of the actors, or if one were reading, the characters, as well as in the spectacle of real life – in the "melodramatic mode" of "physical gestures, political actions, and visual cues," as Elaine Hadley has convincingly argued.[33] And this semiotic display can be located in vocal gesture, as we shall see, even to a greater extent, although this signifying region has been largely neglected in Victorian studies.

Reading character in the features of the face is the work of physiogno-mists as well as audiences, to the extent that these populations differed; one should not overlook the important intersections between this popular Victorian "science" and theatrical/novelistic discourse. People used the same physiognomic criteria to assess fictional characters and their own neighbors. Even the period's most "legitimate" scientist, Charles Darwin, studied the physical expression of emotion in human beings, noting in 1872 that "most of our emotions are so closely connected with their expression that they hardly exist if the body remains passive."[34] The nineteenth-century acting manuals, then, which quantified the passions and instructed practitioners in their invocation, confirmed a significant "scientific" theory. It is no surprise that novelists accepted the authority of the stage.

Dickens, certainly, depended on the semiotic apparati articulated by theatre experts like Henry Siddons; _Nickleby_ and most of Dickens' other novels embody the passions consistently with their manuals. By Siddons' authority, a figure like Ralph Nickleby would typically assume a specific set of attitudes, those believed to represent his reigning emotions – "anger," "hauteur," and "painful recollection" are among the attitudes illustrated by Siddons which could, at various moments in the novel, be ascribed to Ralph. "Hauteur" is represented as a man with an arched spine, prominent chest and stomach, right arm cocked behind the back, right leg turned out and bearing his forward weight, and an erect head with a supercilious expression. "Painful recollection" shows a man facing right, curled slightly forward in a protective gesture, his right arm bent upwards toward his face, hand open-palmed, left arm thrown back behind his body, his feet wide apart and knees bent in a kind of stagger. Ralph's disdain for his country relatives would be registered as "the turning away from [them], or looking at [them] aside, darting a quick glance with a haughty air" (p. 169).

Hablôt Browne represented "Mr. Ralph Nickleby's 'honest' composure" in a plate for the novel,[35] in a fashion that strongly resembles one of Siddons', or somewhat later in the century, Edmund Shaftesbury's dramatic postures;[36] in fact, the entire scene is as stylized and externalized as a tableau – Browne was as indebted to the theatre as Dickens for his visual imagination – with Ralph stage left, legs slightly parted, arms crossed and one wrist tightly clasped as if to suppress some evil impulse, his face averted from the spectacle of Nicholas' honest anger and his eyes "darting a quick glance" into the wings in a highly sinister manner. And later in the novel, Dickens himself casts Ralph in much the same pose: "As he said this, Ralph clenched his right wrist tightly with his left hand, and inclining his head a little on one side, and dropping his chin upon his breast, looked at him whom he addressed with a frowning, sullen face: the picture of a man whom nothing could move or soften."[37] Whether or not Browne was consciously referring to this description when he composed his sketch, the posture he – and Dickens – created for Ralph was a theatrical one; "picture" was another word for "tableau," and thus Ralph as picture carries a double meaning. Victorian readers were prepared for Ralph Nickleby and all of the characters in Dickens' cast, by a theatrical industry which promoted (its legacy from Descartes) a kind of semiotics of the passions, lending a visual/vocal integrity to the character traits which dominate the pages of Victorian novels.

The field of semiotic possibilities into which Dickens' novels were born included strictly delineated verbal stereotypes, which were tied to class, geographic location, and genre (e.g. dialect, patter, aristocratic slurring or clipping, standard English); patterns of physical gesture; sartorial assumptions;[38] even a politics of physical placement – that is, staging – which of course developed in the theatre and presumed certain conditions, like a proscenium frame and frontal viewing audience. Readers of *Oliver Twist,* for example, could assume, indeed were obliged to assume, that Fagin was not an Englishman but some other specimen altogether, with his slightly strange locutions, his occasional but not regular grammatical lapses, and his compulsive repetition of "my dear" in almost every sentence; that the Artful Dodger *was* what might be described as "English," but a specimen of the lower sort, a speaker of street English; and that Mr. Brownlow was a gentleman, a speaker of standard English. They could translate the Beadle's self-importance into a largeness of gesture, a slowness of movement; in Fagin, as in *David Copperfield's* slightly less offensive Uriah Heep, they might expect an oiliness, a creeping and sliding movement, a voice not distinguished or resonant. In scenes which pit the lower sort of scoundrel – Uriah is a good example – against the hero, these readers, brought up on theatre, could visualize the "picture" or *tableau* which so often concluded each act of a nineteenth-century play: hero center stage, scoundrel down-stage, perhaps, and off to one side (in a significantly lower place if the stage was raked), and frozen in the dramatic attitude appropriate to his moral and emotional state. This was how the Victorian public read books, watched plays, and even, I would argue, lived life. What I am describing is essentially a semiotics of theatre and social life. Theatrical signs must be intimately connected to real-life social signs because successful performance depends upon prior agreement, between play-wrights, directors, actors, and audiences, upon the "normative theatri-cal code," as Erika Fischer-Lichte calls it; the various possible contextual meanings of signs.[39] The same may be said, of course, about novelistic signs, to the extent that they differ – and they rarely do, in the nine-teenth century – from theatrical signs. An audience brings its readings of the social world to a play or novel because plays and novels generally reference the moment's mainstream cultural, social, political, and aes-thetic ideas, the "possibilities and strategies of performance" corre-sponding, as Herbert Blau points out,[40] to the varying trends in

Plate 1. *Hauteur.* Plate from Henry Siddons, *Practical Illustrations of Rhetorical Gesture and Action* (1822).

Plate 2. *Painful Recollection.* Plate from Henry Siddons, *Practical Illustrations of Rhetorical Gesture and Action* (1822).

Plate 3. Hablôt K. Browne (Phiz), *Mr. Ralph Nickleby's "Honest Composure."* Original
illustration for Charles Dickens, *Nicholas Nickleby* (1838–9).

hegemonic thinking. That an audience brings its readings of the theatre
to the "real" world is somewhat more surprising, but among Victorians,
in any case, this was true: theatrical signs were received as genuine and
normative – fully legitimate and operative in the social world.

*Nicholas Nickleby*, often staged and itself highly theatrical, demonstrates
the interchangeability of theatrical, literary, and social codes: its irresis-
tability for playwrights and its own heavy reliance on the culture and
signs of the stage are suggestive of a generic breakdown specific to the
nineteenth century, the mutual interdependence between novel and

theatre which I have already described as being peculiarly Victorian.[41] Dickens published the novel serially between April 1838 and October 1839; in 1838 Edward Stirling wrote a play based on it which was produced, along with several other adaptations, before the novel's completion.[42] Stirling's is a simplistic "good-versus-evil" drama, in which unequivocally bad characters work exclusively to undermine their honest counterparts. In this burletta, Ralph Nickleby is implicated in a plot against his son Smike's life ("That half-witted fool still lives, altho' we tried everything" Wackford Squeers informs him, and Ralph replies, "As you value any friendship – never let me hear any news of the brat again – but – his – . . . Death – ha! ha!"); Nicholas acts and speaks with saccharine sweetness; and in case we fail to understand exactly what they are up to, all of the *dramatis personae* periodically break into character-revealing songs. In a sort of ironic regression, Dickens' characters, borrowed from the melodrama and rendered magnificently larger and more complex than their sources, are deflated and returned to their origins. So that when Ralph contemplates the power of money, he does so in a grotesquely simple sung soliloquy, not in the prosily pathological manner of Dickens' villain.

> Money is your friend, is it not?
> Money is your friend, is it not?
> Is it not – is it not?
> Pray tell to me.
> Yes – money money money
> Is your friend.

Although Ralph's song seems infantile and silly, it deserves some notice. Its grotesqueness derives in part from its strange and uncomfortable structure, its metrical and rhythmical uneasiness. This may indicate incompetence, but it also raises some interesting questions about the song's contemporary reception. When we try to scan it, under the assumption that a song, and one almost compulsively, rhythmically repetitive, must scan, we find no metrical design at all, just a random sprinkling of stressed and weak syllables. Practically speaking, it must have been difficult to sing. And, without any hint of what the music sounded like (the score is not printed with the play and probably has not survived), I suspect that this song, at the level of rhythm and perhaps tonality, unsettled the audience, performed the maladjustment it describes. This probably demonstrates the affective power of language and music more than it does a spark of insight on the play-

wright's part: on some basic level this melodrama played on the affec-
tions, as the genre was, of course, meant to do. But its strongest
impressions were made at the level of broad gesture. Stirling employs a
conventional theatrical stereotype with his Ralph Nickleby, who is
foiled at the play's end and slinks off stage swearing revenge. He has
adapted the novel according to the principles of melodrama, employing a set of verbal, physical, and incidental gestures which Victorian
audiences knew how to interpret.

To a large extent Dickens, like most of his literary colleagues, was
using these signs as well, as George Taylor has noted.[43] The idealistic
young hero, the physically threatened heroine, the wicked patriarchal
authority figure, all part and parcel of the standard melodramatic plot,
live and work in *Nicholas Nickleby,* and in virtually all of Dickens' novels.
Yet they transcend the structures of gross melodrama. This has something to do with Dickens' brilliant critical eye and comic sensibility, his
exquisite narrative abilities, his profound understanding of pathos. It
may also be explained generically. In spite of that generic conflation
characteristic of the nineteenth century, novels and plays did, of course,
sustain certain generic integrities. For example, the practice of fiction
writing, unlike the practice of melodrama, allows a padding of even the
commonest stock characters with real human flesh. Perhaps most importantly, the codes of the novel generally accommodate – in fact, in the
nineteenth century, virtually mandated – the use of metaphor and
simile. Conversely, nineteenth-century dramatic practice insisted on a
kind of semiotic transparency, a direct relationship between gesture, for
example, and the passion or personality trait it claimed to represent – in
other words, a sort of antimetaphoric metaphoring. In theatre, then,
one had merely the paradox of "truthfully" feigned situations, with little
or no poetry, or irony, or fancy (heightened language was employed, but
only as a grace note on the text, a conventional marker of social or moral
elevation); in fiction, one had theatre with complications – with the
richness and slipperiness, and in the case of Dickens the sheer beauty, of
metaphoric language.

But Victorian readers conflated fictional and theatrical codes despite
these significant generic differences. This surely happened when people
read *Nickleby.* Those who had seen Stirling's adaptation, for example,
saw his broadly villainous Ralph Nickleby played against Dickens'
psychologically complicated character, a man with a past, a subject of
stories, a father, one whose obsessions and anger may be ultimately
understood if not forgiven.